THE
PIED
PIPER
OF HAMELIN

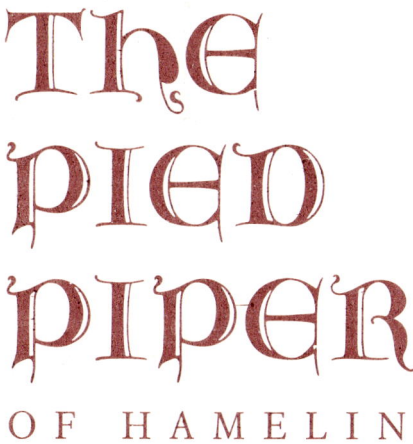

The Pied Piper

OF HAMELIN

BY ROBERT BROWNING

REVISED AND ILLUSTRATED BY TERRY SMALL

GULLIVER BOOKS
HARCOURT BRACE JOVANOVICH
SAN DIEGO   NEW YORK   LONDON

HBJ

Copyright © 1988 by Terry Small

All rights reserved.
No part of this publication may be reproduced
or transmitted in any form or by any means,
electronic or mechanical, including photocopy, recording,
or any information storage and retrieval system,
without permission in writing from the publisher.

Requests for permission to make copies of
any part of the work should be mailed to:
Permissions, Harcourt Brace Jovanovich, Publishers,
Orlando, Florida 32887.

Library of Congress Cataloging-in-Publication Data

Small, Terry.
The Pied Piper of Hamelin/revised and
illustrated by Terry Small.—1st ed.
    p.   cm.
Based on the version by Robert Browning.
"Gulliver books."
Summary: The Pied Piper pipes the village free of rats,
and when the villagers refuse to pay him for the
service he exacts a terrible revenge.
ISBN 0-15-200566-8
1. Pied Piper of Hamelin (Legendary character)—Juvenile poetry.
2. Children's poetry, American. [1. Pied Piper of Hamelin
(Legendary character)—Poetry. 2. Folklore—Germany
(West)—Hameln—Poetry.
3. American poetry.]
I. Browning, Robert, 1812-1889.
Pied Piper of Hamelin. II. Title.
PS3569.M288P5   1988   811'.54—dc 19

Printed in the United States of America
First edition
A B C D E

To Adele Edwards Small
— T.S.

PREFACE

The origin of the Pied Piper legend is lost in the dim twilight of the Middle Ages. It first surfaces in a manuscript out of Lüneburg, Germany, dating back to about 1430 to 1450, in which a piper is said to have lured 130 children out of the town of Hameln in the province of Hanover. This sudden disappearance of the young, supposed to have occurred in 1284, was call the *Exodus Hamelensis*. Onto this mysterious event storytellers of the following century grafted a character from German folklore, the more or less demonic Rattenfänger or "rat-catcher," who is still being puzzled over by modern researchers.

Though the historical basis of the legend is thus obscured by fantasy, it has not deterred scholars from seeking a plausible explanation. Some have imagined that the story reflects the departure of Hameln's young men at the bidding of a certain bishop, who brought them as colonists to Moravia in Czechoslovakia. Others have seen in the story a medieval migration from Germany to the Polish region of Pomerania. Whether or not there is truth in these suggestions, it seems certain that the legend as we now have it draws inspiration from three significant events of the thirteenth through the fifteenth centuries.

First, the Children's Crusade of 1212 was hatched in Germany when a boy, Nicolas of Köln, who succeeded in leading twenty thousand young followers as far as Italy in hopes of crossing the sea dry-shod to reclaim Jerusalem from the Moslem infidels. The crusade was a miserable and tragic failure, and most of the children never saw their homes again. Second, the bubonic plague—known as the Black Death—swept across Europe between 1346 and 1361 in conjunction with the rapid increase in population of the black rat as it migrated from Asia. An estimated one-quarter to one-third of the medieval population was wiped out, leaving whole towns and districts depopulated. And third, those who survived the crusades and the plague were soon to encounter that strange, mystical race of wandering musicians and sorcerers whom they called "Egyptians" and we know as Gypsies. By 1417 the mysterious foreigners had crossed Germany to its western parts; five years later they appeared at Bologna and in 1427 were camped outside the gates of Paris. The legendary Pied Piper—with his magic flute, outlandish dress, and shrewd business proposition—embodies the traditional attributes of the gypsy.

In the course of the last seven centuries, the Pied Piper legend has lost none of its charm and mystery. It has been treated dozens of times in story, verse, song, and drama by a host of writers including the German literary giant Johann Wolfgang von Goethe, whose words have even been set to music.

But the best known of all versions is by the English poet Robert Browning.

From early childhood, Robert Browning seemed destined to produce such a masterpiece. His father, a frustrated artist and writer who had turned his energies to collecting rare and beautiful books, early on steered his young son to a literary career. Among the hundreds of volumes that lined the walls of the family home were at least two that recorded the tale—in English—of the Pied Piper.

Mr. Browning, Sr., actually began to write and illustrate an early version of the story, which he graciously abandoned after his son started work on the same subject.

In May 1842, at age thirty, Robert Browning composed "The Pied Piper of Hamelin" to amuse Willie Macready, the son of his friend actor William Charles Macready. The poem was meant to give the boy something to illustrate while confined to his sickbed. In fact, young Macready spent weeks producing some "delightfully naive" pictures that today are part of the Browning Collection at Baylor University.[1]

Browning never considered his poem a serious work. It was included in his *Dramatic Lyrics*, where it attracted no critical notice whatever, and it appeared in his series *Bells and Pomegranates* only because the printer needed a few more pages of text to fill out the volume. Generations of children and adults have handed down a different verdict, however, and Robert Browning, with keen insight and clever verse, has succeeded in raising an obscure folktale to the status of a children's classic. It should be noted that in so doing the poet has taken liberties with the tale's few solid facts: He transported Hamelin (with an extra syllable) to the province of Brunswick[2] and transferred the exodus itself to the year 1376. No matter: that is how legends grow.

A NOTE ON THIS REVISION

It is a dangerous thing to tamper with the classics. Yet even in Browning's own day—and often since—he has been accused of a profound obscurity, both in language and in thought. He has his defenders, of course, though even they recognize that his poetry is hardly light reading. Browning loved to twist syntax, rhythm, and accent to achieve improbable (some would say impossible) rhymes, and he was fond of sprinkling his work with obsolete words and arcane references. Modern readers would wince at his rhyming "promise" with "from mice" and would probably shrug helplessly at a phrase like "bate a stiver."[3] For this reason I have undertaken to revise the poet's words without, I hope, doing violence to the poem. I have attempted to retain his rhyme and rhythm wherever possible and to make only such changes as I deemed necessary to keep the story readily understandable to modern ears. In doing so, I hope to make the Pied Piper legend familiar to a whole new generation of readers.

Terry Small
1988

NOTES

1. Frances Winwar, *The Immortal Lovers*, 99, footnote 2. New York: Harper & Bros., 1950.

2. In the present revision, the town has been returned to its original province.

3. These words and phrases have been extracted from Robert Browning's original version of "The Piped Piper of Hamelin."

THE
PIED
PIPER
OF HAMELIN

Hamelin Town's in Hanover,
And round about those parts
The river Weser, deep and wide,
Washes its wall on the southern side;
A pleasanter spot you never spied.
But when my story starts,
At least six hundred years ago,
To see the townsfolk suffer so
From rats would break your hearts.

Rats!
They fought the dogs and killed the cats,
And bit the babies in the cradles,
And ate the cheeses out of the vats,
And licked the soup from the cooks' own ladles,
Split open kegs of fish and fats,
Made nests inside men's Sunday hats,
And even spoiled the women's chats
By drowning their speaking
With shrieking and squeaking
In fifty different sharps and flats.

At last the people all came flocking,
Shouting in the great Town Hall:
"Our Council's attitude is shocking!
High you sit and far you'll fall.
To think we buy fine gowns of ermine
For dolts who can't or won't determine
How to rid us of our vermin!

You're old and fat and still expect
Your furry robes to buy respect!
Well, wake up! Give your brains a racking!
Find the remedy we're lacking
Or, sure as fate, we'll send you packing!"
Such words alarmed the Mayor this day
And left the Council in dismay.

They sat in silence an hour long
　Until the Mayor spoke up to say,
"I'd sell my fur coat for a song;
I wish I lived a mile away!
How simple to say 'Go rack your brain'—
My poor head aches from all the strain,
I've scratched it so, and all in vain.
Oh, for a trap, a trap, a trap!"
And just as his brain was about to snap
He heard at the door a gentle tap.

"Bless me!" cried the Mayor. "What's that?"
With his Council there he sat,
Looking little, though wondrous fat:
His eyes were dull in resignation,
Never bright with expectation
(Except at noon when his growling tummy
Craved turtle soup, all green and gummy.)
"Only a scraping of shoes on the mat?
Anything like the sound of a rat
Makes my heart go pit-a-pat!"

"Come in!" the Mayor cried, looking bigger:
And in did come the strangest figure!
His odd long coat from heel to head
Was half of yellow and half of red,
And he himself was tall and thin,
With sharp blue eyes, each like a pin,
And light loose hair, yet swarthy skin,
No tuft on cheek nor beard on chin,
But lips where smiles went out and in:
There was no guessing his origin.

And no one could enough admire
The tall man and his quaint attire.
Said one, "It's like my great-grandsire,
Rising up at the Trumpet of Doom
Had walked this way from his painted tomb!"

He stepped up to the council table
And said, "Your honors, I am able
By secret magic to enchant
All creatures living beneath the sun
That creep or swim or fly or run.
What I can do most wizards can't.
Chiefly I reserve my charm
For creatures that'll do you harm—
The mole and toad, the newt and viper—
And people call me the Pied Piper."

(And here they noticed round his neck
A scarf of red and yellow stripe
To match his coat of the selfsame check.
And at the scarf's end hung a pipe;
And his fingers, they noticed, were always straying
As if impatient to be playing
Upon this pipe, as low it dangled
Over his garment so old-fangled.)

"Though some," he said, "may smarter be,
Last June I was in Tartary
And saved the Khan from swarms of gnats;
And I kept the Nizam's quarter free
Of a monstrous brood of vampire bats:
Pests like those my charm bewilders.
So if I rid your town of rats
Will you give me a thousand guilders?"
"Not one but *fifty* thousand is fair!"
Exclaimed the Council and the Mayor.

Into the street the Piper stepped,
Smiling first a little smile,
As if he knew what magic slept
In his still pipe all the while,
For there his secret spells were kept.
Then blowing soft, his lips he wrinkled,
And green and blue his sharp eyes twinkled
Like candle flames where salt is sprinkled.

Before three notes of the pipe came fluttering
You heard a sound like armies muttering,
And the muttering grew to a grumbling,
And the grumbling grew to a mighty rumbling,
And out of the houses the rats came tumbling.

Great rats, small rats, lean rats, brawny rats,
Brown rats, black rats, gray rats, tawny rats,
Grave old plodders, gay young friskers,
Fathers, mothers, uncles, cousins,
Cocking tails and pointing whiskers,
Families by tens and dozens,
Brothers, sisters, husbands, wives
Followed the Piper for their lives.

From street to street he piped advancing,
And step for step they followed dancing,
Until at the water's edge they dived
And perished in the river;
Except one bold swimmer who survived
By desperate strokes and self-control
And stood at last with a shake and a shiver
To tell his tale in a Ratland hole.

Said he, "The first shrill notes of the pipe
Reminded me of scraping tripe,
And crushing apples, wondrous ripe,
In cider presses of some type;
And dragging aside the pickle tub-boards,
And pushing ajar the candy cupboards,
And popping the corks of whale-oil flasks,
And breaking the hoops of butter casks;

And I could swear I heard a voice
(None sweeter raised in church or chantry)
Calling out, 'Oh rats, rejoice!
The world is one vast open pantry!
So munch and crunch and take your brunch,
Breakfast, supper, dinner, lunch!'
And there a cask of sugar punch,
Already opened by a bunch
Of us, stood scarce an inch before me:
Just as it seemed to say 'Come, pour me!'
I found the Weser rolling o'er me."

You should have heard the Hamelin people
Ringing the bells till they rocked the steeple.
"Go," cried the Mayor, "and get long poles,
Poke out the nests, block up the holes!
Consult with carpenters and builders
So all those rats will leave no trace—"
When suddenly the Piper's face
Popped up there in the marketplace,
With, "First, if you please, my thousand guilders."

A thousand guilders! The Mayor looked blue;
So did his Council members, too.
For all their banquets went so well
With jugs of claret, hock, Moselle,
And half that money would replenish
Their cellar's biggest cask of Rhenish.
To pay this sum to a wandering fellow
With a gypsy coat of red and yellow!

"Besides," said the Mayor with a knowing wink,
"Our business was done at the river's brink;
We saw with our eyes the vermin sink,
And what's dead can't come to life, I think.
So, friend, we're not the folks to shrink
From the duty of giving you something to drink,
And a handful of coins to put in your cloak;
But as for the guilders of which we spoke,
You know very well it was only a joke.
Besides, our losses have made us thrifty;
A thousand guilders? No! Take fifty."

The Piper's face fell, and he cried,
"No trifling! I can't wait, beside!
I've promised to go as a dinner guest
To Baghdad, to accept the best
Of the Head Cook's soup (that's all he's rich in),
Because I delivered the Caliph's kitchen
From a nest of scorpions in the rice.
With him the bargain was precise;
With you, don't think I'll cut my price!
And folks who put me in a passion
May find me pipe in another fashion!"

The Mayor cried back, "How would it look,
Me treated worse than a common Cook?
Insulted by a lazy goat
With idle pipe and checkered coat!
You threaten us, fellow? Do your worst!
Blow your pipe there till you burst!"

Once more he stepped into the street
And to his lips again
Laid his long pipe of smooth straight cane.
Before he blew three notes (so sweet
And soft, and yet so cunning),
There was a rustling that seemed like a bustling
Of merry crowds justling at pitching and hustling.
Small feet were pattering, wooden shoes clattering,
Little hands clapping and little tongues chattering,
And, like fowls on a farm when barley is scattering,
Out came the children running.

All the little boys and girls,
With rosy cheeks and flaxen curls,
And sparkling eyes and teeth like pearls,
Tripping and skipping, ran merrily after
The wonderful music, with shouting and laughter.

The Mayor was still, and the Council stood
As if they were changed into blocks of wood.
Unable to move a step or cry
To the children merrily skipping by,
They could only follow with the eye
That joyous crowd at the Piper's back.
But how the Council's thoughts turned black
And the wretched Mayor's bosom beat
When the Piper turned from the High Street
To where the Weser rolled its waters
Right in the way of their sons and daughters!

However, he turned from South to West
And up to Koppelberg Hill progressed,
And after him the children pressed.
Great was the joy in every breast:
"He never can cross that mighty top!
He's forced to let the piping drop,
And we shall see our children stop!"

But lo! As they reached the mountain's side
A wondrous portal opened wide,
As if a cavern was suddenly hollowed;
And the Piper advanced and the children followed,
And when all were in to the very last,
The door in the mountainside shut fast.
Did I say all? No! One was lame
And could not dance the whole of the way;
And in later years he used to blame
His sadness on that very day:
"Our town is dull since my playmates left!
I can't forget that I'm bereft
Of all the pleasant sights they see,
Which the Piper also promised me.

For he led us, he said, to a joyous land,
Outside of town but near at hand,
Where waters gushed and fruit trees grew,
And flowers put forth a fairer hue,
And everything was strange and new.
The sparrows were brighter than peacocks here,
And their dogs outran our swiftest deer,
And honeybees had lost their stings,
And horses were born with eagles' wings;

And just as I became assured
My lame foot would be speedily cured,
The music stopped, and I stood still
And found myself outside the hill,
Left alone against my will,
To go on limping as before
And never hear of that country more!"

Alas, alas for Hamelin!
Some folk recalled they'd heard before
A verse which says that heaven's door
Opens up to the rich no more
Than the needle's eye lets a camel in!

The Mayor sent East, West, North, and South
To offer the Piper by word of mouth,
Wherever men by chance should find him,
Silver and gold to his heart's content,
If he'd only return the way he went
And bring the children all behind him.

But when they saw it was a lost endeavor,
And Piper and dancers were gone forever,
They made a decree that lawyers never
Could any parchment certify
Unless these words too should appear
After the day of the month and year:
"And so long after what happened here
On the twenty-second of July
Thirteen hundred and seventy-six."

And the better in memory to fix
The path of the children's last retreat,
They call that place Pied Piper Street,
Where anyone playing a pipe or drum
Was driven back the way he'd come;
Nor did they allow an inn or tavern
To spill forth joy on a street so solemn.

But opposite the place of the cavern
They wrote the story on a column,
And on the great church window painted
A scene to make the world acquainted
With how their children were stolen away,
And there it stands to this very day.

And I must not omit to say
That in Transylvania there's a tribe
With such outlandish ways and dress
They cause their neighbors much distress:
This alien people still describe
How their fathers and mothers once had risen
Out of some subterranean prison,
Lured there by some sleight of hand
Long ago in a mighty band
From Hamelin Town in Hanover land,
But how or why they don't understand.

And so, dear friends, let us not be gripers
In dealing with people—especially pipers!
Sometimes it's not in our power to choose
Just what we keep and what we lose.
And those who can't see beyond the cost
Should consider this tale and what was lost.
It ought to sway even a doubting Thomas:
Better to lose your purse and keep your promise!

The illustrations in this book were done in pen and ink.

The display type was set in Lombardic Initials.

The text type was set in Simoncini Garamond.

Composition by Thompson Type, San Diego, California

Printed and bound by Horowitz/Rae Book Manufacturers, Inc., Fairfield, New Jersey

Production supervision by Warren Wallerstein and Ginger Boyer

Designed by Michael Farmer

DISCARD

J821 B
BROWNING, ROBERT, 1812-1889.

THE PIED PIPER OF HAMELIN

CHILDREN'S ROOM

WHITE PLAINS PUBLIC LIBRARY

White Plains, N. Y.

AUG 31 1989